WELCOME TO MY COUNTRY

Welcome to the
USA

Gareth Stevens Publishing
A WORLD ALMANAC EDUCATION GROUP COMPANY

Written by
NICOLE FRANK/ELIZABETH BERG

Designed by
LOO CHUAN MING

Picture research by
SUSAN JANE MANUEL

First published in North America in 2000 by
Gareth Stevens Publishing
A World Almanac Education Group Company
1555 North RiverCenter Drive, Suite 201
Milwaukee, Wisconsin 53212 USA

For a free color catalog describing
Gareth Stevens' list of high-quality books
and multimedia programs, call
1-800-542-2595 (USA) or
1-800-461-9120 (CANADA).
Gareth Stevens Publishing's
Fax: (414) 225-0377.

© **TIMES MEDIA PRIVATE LIMITED 2000**
Originated and designed by
Times Editions
an imprint of Times Media Private Limited
Times Centre, 1 New Industrial Road
Singapore 536196
http://www.timesone.com.sg/te

Library of Congress Cataloging-in-Publication Data

Frank, Nicole.
Welcome to the USA / Nicole Frank and Elizabeth Berg.
p. cm. — (Welcome to my country)
Includes bibliographical references and index.
Summary: An overview of the geography, history, government,
economy, people, and culture of the United States.
ISBN 0-8368-2513-6 (lib. bdg.)
1. United States—Juvenile literature. [1. United States.] I. Berg,
Elizabeth, 1953– II. Title. III. Series.
E156.F7   2000
973—dc21   99-087934

Printed in Malaysia

1 2 3 4 5 6 7 8 9 04 03 02 01 00

PICTURE CREDITS
Bes Stock: 23, 24
Camera Press: 14, 16, 30
Focus Team: 3 (center), 22
Haga Library: 21, 32 (bottom), 35,
    39 (both)
Blaine Harrington: 1, 6, 20, 25, 36, 37, 45
HBL Network: Cover, 11 (bottom), 13, 17,
    18, 29 (top), 32 (top)
Dave G. Houser: 3 (top), 5, 8 (top), 9
    (both), 10, 19
The Hutchison Library: 26, 27, 31 (bottom),
    33, 34
International Photobank: 2, 4, 7, 8 (bottom)
North Wind Picture Archives: 3 (bottom),
    15 (all), 28, 29 (bottom)
Christine Osborne: 38, 40, 41 (both)
Topham Picturepoint: 31 (top)
Vision Photo Agency: 12
Horst Von Irmer: 11 (top)

Digital Scanning by Superskill Graphics Pte Ltd

Contents

Words that appear in the glossary are printed in **boldface** type the first time they occur in the text.

4

Welcome to the USA!

The United States is a country of contrasts — crowded cities and barren wilderness and majestic riches and **debilitating** poverty. The great size of the United States has always provided new frontiers to explore. Let's learn about the United States and the many ethnic groups that populate the country.

Opposite: San Francisco's famous trolley cars inch their way up the city's hills.

Below: Americans enjoy camping and fishing in the wilderness.

The Flag of the United States

The American flag, called the Stars and Stripes, was adopted in 1777, when the United States became independent. The red and white stripes represent America's thirteen original colonies. Each star represents one of the fifty states.

The Land

The fourth largest country in the world, the United States consists of fifty states, including Alaska, to the north of Canada, and Hawaii, which lies in the Pacific Ocean. The forty-eight **contiguous** states cover 3,096,107 square miles (8,018,917 square kilometers). They are bordered by the Atlantic and Pacific Oceans, Canada, and Mexico.

Below: Jackson Lake is surrounded by a breathtaking view of Wyoming's Teton mountain range. The lake and mountains teem with wildlife, including fish, buffalo, antelope, and elk.

Left: The Grand Canyon's majestic gorge was carved out by the winding Colorado River. A natural wonder of the world, the Grand Canyon is 277 miles (446 km) long and 18 miles (29 km) wide. Visitors can drive, hike, raft, and ride mules through the canyon.

The United States has a variety of climates and terrains, including forested coastal plains, the Appalachian Mountains, central plains, the Rocky Mountains, western plateaus, and the Pacific ranges.

The six great rivers of the United States are the Mississippi, Missouri, Ohio, Columbia, Colorado, and Rio Grande. They are used for trade, fishing, **irrigation**, and hydroelectric power.

Climate

Above: The leaves of **deciduous** trees turn red, orange, and gold in autumn.

Climate in the United States ranges from the wet Pacific Northwest to the arid deserts of Arizona, and from the bitter cold of North Dakota to tropical Florida.

Much of the United States enjoys four seasons annually. Alaska, however, is cold most of the year, and the western coast remains mild all year. The southwestern deserts are hot during the day, but cool at night.

Plants and Animals

The United States has a large variety of flora and fauna. The southeastern region is famous for its fruit trees, while the southwestern region has desert-type vegetation. Stunning, giant redwood trees grow along the northwestern coast.

Animals thrive in the American wilderness. Bears live in national parks, and deer inhabit various forested areas.

Above: The Everglades of Florida are packed with plants and animals. Both crocodiles and alligators make their homes in this swampy area.

Left: The bald eagle, noted for its power and beauty, is the national bird of the United States. It is considered a threatened species and lives along rivers and lakes.

Opposite, below: Arizona's Sonora Desert is dotted with large cacti, including the saguaro cactus, which can grow to 40 feet (12 meters).

History

The first inhabitants of North America arrived about 25,000 years ago. European explorer Christopher Columbus arrived in this New World in 1492, followed by other colonists.

In 1775, the colonists became unhappy with British rule, which led to the Revolutionary War. The colonies declared themselves independent on July 4, 1776. They defeated the British in 1781. General George Washington became the first president.

Above:
In the early 1800s, pioneers headed west, traveling in groups along dangerous and unfamiliar trails. These men reenact the pioneers' crossing of the Snake River.

Left: Railroads transported people and goods to the western frontier, helping the region grow and prosper. In 1869, the first transcontinental railway was completed in Promontory, Utah.

Below: Between 1860 and 1890, about fifty thousand Native Americans were killed by settlers and by diseases. Indians were forced to live on **reservations**, where they have found it difficult to keep native traditions alive.

Territorial Expansion

In 1803, the United States doubled in size when it acquired the Louisiana Territory. In 1848, it won the Mexican War, and Mexico handed over land that extended from Texas to the Pacific, including California.

Civil War

By the 1850s, the northeastern states were industrialized, while southeastern states were agricultural. African slaves labored on farms and plantations in the south. In 1861, tension between the north and the south led to the Civil War. Four years later, the northern states won the war and slavery was abolished.

Below:
The southern Confederate army was small, but it put up a good fight in the Civil War. Although it beat the northern Union army at the battle of Chickamauga Creek in Georgia, the south was forced to surrender on April 9, 1865.

Left: World War II was the first time aircraft carriers were used as combat vessels. The *Independence* was built after the war and is able to carry more equipment than earlier models. Today, many carriers have missiles on board.

An Emerging World Power

The United States won new territories in 1898. In 1917, the country entered World War I. A decade of prosperity followed, ending with the 1929 stock market crash and the **Great Depression**. The United States entered World War II in 1941 and emerged a world power.

Fighting the Cold War

After World War II, relations between the United States and the Soviet Union became strained. The two nations entered the Cold War, a period of nonviolent hostility with the threat of nuclear war. The United States actively fought communism in the Korean and Vietnam Wars. The Cold War ended in 1991, when the Soviet Union collapsed. Today, the United States exerts great influence in the global economy and in the international community.

Below: The Vietnam War was a time of tension and division in the United States. Many people disapproved of America's involvement in the war and the death of American soldiers.

Thomas Jefferson (1743–1826)

Before his two terms as president, Thomas Jefferson wrote the Declaration of Independence and served as the governor of Virginia, U.S. minister to France, secretary of state, and vice president.

Thomas Jefferson

Abraham Lincoln (1809–1865)

Abraham Lincoln became president in 1860. The Civil War began in 1861. As the country's commander-in-chief, Lincoln helped lead the north to victory. He was assassinated five days after the war ended.

Abraham Lincoln

Elizabeth Cady Stanton (1815–1902)

Elizabeth Cady Stanton helped organize the first women's rights convention in New York. Later, she copublished a newspaper promoting women's rights. Stanton **advocated** coeducation and liberal divorce laws.

Elizabeth Cady Stanton

Government and the Economy

Democracy in Action

A federal democracy was established under the U.S. Constitution. Power is divided between the state and national governments. The executive, judicial, and legislative branches form the national government. Each branch checks the other two to balance power.

Below: President Bill Clinton delivers his State of the Union address to Congress. This speech outlines points the president thinks lawmakers should consider in their next session.

The Bill of Rights

The Bill of Rights, the first ten amendments to the Constitution, guarantees Americans certain freedoms, including freedom of religion, speech, and the press. Seventeen more amendments have been added since 1791, for a total of twenty-seven today.

Economy

The success of the U.S. economy is a result of its **adaptability** to new technologies. In the late 1800s, the country moved from an agricultural to an industrial economic base.

Industry declined when cheaper goods from other countries threatened U.S. manufacturing. Services now keep the economy going, and the computer industry continues to grow.

Above: Labor costs are cheaper overseas. To keep manufacturing jobs in the United States, some American manufacturers and foreign competitors have come up with **novel** solutions. For example, at this Toyota plant, a Japanese company, cars are assembled by local American workers and sold domestically.

The United States is rich in natural resources. Coal, natural gas, crude oil, iron ore, uranium, gold, and silver are just some of the abundant resources found here.

The United States leads the world in the production of agricultural products. Crops grown in the United States feed the United States and one-sixth of the world. Although only 4 percent of Americans work in the farming industry, 43 percent of the land is farmland.

Below: An American invention, the combine efficiently harvests crops.

People and Lifestyle

The American population is over 272 million — 30 percent live in cities and 45 percent in suburbs. A decreasing city population has led to **deterioration** and traffic congestion because more and more people commute from the suburbs to workplaces in the cities.

Left: Immigrants from around the world have made their homes in the United States. The population is estimated to be 387 million by the year 2050, with an estimated 81 million people being of mixed racial heritage.

A Land of Immigrants

The United States is a land of immigrants, with a variety of races and nationalities. As the country grew, people arrived from all over the world and formed communities of their own, such as Little Italy in New York. Today, most immigrants have adopted an American way of life.

Home Sweet Home

The kitchen's informal atmosphere provides a comfortable place for family members to talk. Barbecues with family and friends are common on weekends.

Above: Hayrides are a fun pastime in the rural areas of the United States.

Family Time

Most Americans do not live in their hometowns permanently. Many move away when they go to college, find work, or get married. Unlike in other cultures, **extended families** are rare, and **nuclear families** are the norm.

Many American families now include two working parents. The increasing rate of divorce has resulted in more single-parent families.

The Road to Adulthood

Individuality is very important in American culture. Young people in America are expected to become more independent as they get older, and they are expected to get part-time jobs to earn pocket money. Learning to drive is another step toward independence. Americans tend to leave home between the ages of eighteen and twenty-one.

Below: Many Americans enjoy outdoor activities, such as hiking.

Education

American children must attend primary and secondary school. Most students go to public schools. Children attend kindergarten at age five before going

on to primary school. Middle school begins in the fifth or sixth grade. High school begins in the eighth or ninth grade. Students learn history, reading, science, mathematics, and other subjects. Most students graduate high school at age eighteen.

Above:
Kindergarten helps prepare students for primary school.

Thirty-four percent of high school graduates attend college. Every state has its own public universities, but there are also many private universities. An undergraduate degree typically takes four years. Many students return to college to earn an advanced degree.

Religion

Over one thousand religions are practiced in the United States. The Bill of Rights guarantees freedom of religion, and the government does not involve itself in religious matters.

Religious Diversity

Fifty-three percent of Americans are Protestants. Baptists, Lutherans, and Methodists are all Protestants. Roman Catholics make up 26 percent of the population. In the nineteenth and

Below: Lively singing can be heard in many African-American church services.

twentieth centuries, immigration from Ireland, Italy, and Mexico led to an increase in the Catholic population.

Jews, Muslims, and Eastern Orthodox Christians each represent 2 percent of the population. Islam is growing rapidly in the United States, with seven million followers.

Language

The basic grammar and usage of American English can be attributed to Noah Webster, who developed American grammar. Webster created a **linguistic** identity based on spoken English. He created new grammatical rules, disregarding many old British English rules.

Above: In 1828, Noah Webster (1758–1843) published *An American Dictionary of the English Language.* He used American spelling in the dictionary.

A Rich Written History

The New World presented an ideal setting for many early American authors. Washington Irving became the country's first short story writer. Edgar Allan Poe, who wrote the poem "The Raven," is famous for his dark, mysterious tales. Herman Melville, Mark Twain, and Henry David Thoreau all excelled at different writing styles.

Ernest Hemingway, William Faulkner, and Toni Morrison have won the Nobel Prize for Literature.

Master Poets

Walt Whitman, Emily Dickinson, T. S. Eliot, Robert Frost, and Maya Angelou have all left their mark on American poetry. Theodore Geisel, better known as Dr. Seuss, is famous for his books for children, such as *The Cat in the Hat*.

Above: Samuel Langhorne Clemens, better known as Mark Twain, wrote several famous books, such as *The Prince and the Pauper, Life on the Mississippi, The Adventures of Tom Sawyer,* and *The Adventures of Huckleberry Finn.*

Left: Washington Irving wrote *Rip Van Winkle,* a story about a man who sleeps for twenty years and awakens to find the United States an independent country.

Arts

American Visual Artists

American art was dominated by European influences until 1825. After World War II, **abstract expressionism** emerged. Artists explored the physical act of painting. In the 1960s, artists such as Andy Warhol and Jasper Johns used photographs, objects, and other **media** to depict popular culture.

Left: Andy Warhol (1928–1987) was at the forefront of the Pop Art movement, which began as a **criticism** of **commercialism** in American culture. Warhol created bold paintings and experimental films.

Reaching for the Sky

American architect Louis Sullivan created the world's first skyscrapers. Frank Lloyd Wright, famous for designing the Guggenheim Museum, used big, open spaces and **incorporated** the setting into the design. The glass-box look, **post-modernism**, and other architectural styles have also flourished in the United States.

Lyrics and Tunes

Ethnic groups in the United States have contributed to American musical history. African-Americans provided jazz, blues, and rock 'n' roll. In the 1920s, the British, who settled in the Appalachian Mountains, developed country and western music. One of America's best loved composers is George Gershwin, who wrote *Porgy and Bess*. Broadway in New York City is the home of many famous musicals.

Above: Elvis Aaron Presley was born in 1935. Revered as "The King" of American rock 'n' roll, Elvis died in 1977. His Memphis home, Graceland, is visited by thousands of people every year.

Left: New Orleans' Preservation Hall is a famous jazz club. Jazz tunes, with their characteristic **improvisation**, are never played the same way twice. Americans Duke Ellington, Louis Armstrong, and Billie Holiday are famous jazz greats.

May I Have This Dance?

Several dances originated in the United States. Square dance, the most popular folk dance in the country, and modern dance are two uniquely American dances. Alvin Ailey combined African dance and classical ballet.

Leisure

Above: Americans love camping. This family roasts marshmallows over an open fire.

Watching television, cooking, and using the computer are popular American pastimes. Teenagers enjoy spending time going to the movies, the mall, and concerts. Many Americans also enjoy dancing, reading, gardening, sewing, and painting.

Americans also like to keep active. Swimming, golf, and tennis are popular sports. In winter, children enjoy making snowmen and sledding.

Sports Fans

Popular team sports in the United States include baseball, basketball, and football. Many Americans participate in local sports leagues and watch their favorite teams play on television or at a stadium. Millions, for example, follow baseball's annual World Series.

For those who are lucky enough to attend, baseball games are a special treat. Hot dogs, cotton candy, and peanuts are all part of the experience!

Below: Beaches, such as Hawaii's famous Waikiki Beach, attract hundreds of people daily. Popular beach activities include swimming, surfing, volleyball, and picnicking.

Play Ball!

American football is based on English rugby. Baseball evolved from the British game of rounders.

Little League is an organization of baseball teams for children aged eight to twelve. Girls were admitted beginning in 1974. Most communities have Little League teams, which are supported by the players' parents. Weekend games bring families together.

Below: School and community-sponsored sports teams provide American children with opportunities to participate.

The Great Outdoors

The vast outdoors of the United States allows Americans to enjoy leisure activities such as hiking, camping, and canoeing. National parks and public recreational facilities are perfect places for outdoor activities. Highways are often congested on Friday nights when city dwellers head for recreation spots outside the city.

Festivals and Holidays

Independence Day is celebrated on July 4, with picnics and fireworks. Thanksgiving, held in November, began when European settlers celebrated their first year in the New World by feasting with Native Americans.

Christmas is a Christian holiday and a time when families sing carols, attend church, and decorate Christmas trees.

Easter, another Christian holiday, is celebrated with church, elaborate dinners, and Easter egg hunts.

Each ethnic group has its own festivals — Jewish people celebrate Hanukkah, while African-Americans celebrate Juneteenth Day and Kwanza.

Above: Carved pumpkins, called jack-o'-lanterns, often light the way for costumed children as they go from house to house collecting candy on Halloween night.

Left: Thanksgiving is celebrated on the fourth Thursday of November. Thousands of people attend New York City's famous parade, and millions more watch this spectacular parade on television.

Food

Immigrants have greatly influenced American cuisine. Native Americans introduced European settlers to wild game and native plants. English cooking techniques were then used to prepare **indigenous** ingredients. Traditional American dishes incorporate the culinary styles of many immigrant groups.

Below:
Delicatessens sell prepared meats and cheeses. Most of these stores have lunch counters where customers can enjoy hot soup and sandwiches.

Most Americans begin their days with a light breakfast of toast or cereal. Pancakes are a favorite breakfast dish. A typical lunchtime meal includes a sandwich, soup, or salad. Dinner is usually the biggest meal of the day.

Each region of the United States has its own specialties. New England is famous for Boston baked beans and clam chowder, a soup made from clams and cream. New York City serves a selection of **kosher food**, which follows Jewish dietary laws. **Grits** and fried chicken are southern specialties.

USA

A   **B**   **C**   **D**

1

CANADA

WASHINGTON

OREGON

IDAHO

MONTANA

NORTH DAKOTA

MINNESOTA

2

NEVADA

WYOMING

SOUTH DAKOTA

WISCONSIN

CALIFORNIA

San Francisco

UTAH

COLORADO

NEBRASKA

IOWA

KANSAS

MISSOURI

ILLINOI

3

PACIFIC OCEAN

ARIZONA

NEW MEXICO

OKLAHOMA

ARKANSAS

Memp

MISSISSIPPI

TEXAS

LOUISIANA

New Orlear

Legend:
- ──── International Boundary
- ──── State Boundary
- ■ Capital
- ● City
- ～ River

4

MEXICO

5

Mt. McKinley
(20,320 ft/6,194 m)

ALASKA

HAWAII

PUERTO RICO

42

Alabama E3
Alaska A5
Arizona B3
Arkansas D3
Atlantic Ocean F2–F4

California A2–A3
Canada A1–F1
Colorado B2–C2
Connecticut F2
Cuba E5–F5

Delaware F2

Florida E4

Georgia E3

Hawaii B5

Idaho B2
Illinois D2
Indiana E2
Iowa D2

Kansas C3
Kentucky E3

Louisiana D4

Maine F1
Maryland F2
Massachusetts F2
Memphis D3
Mexico B3–C5
Michigan E2
Minnesota D1
Mississippi D3
Missouri D3
Montana B1–C1

Mt. McKinley A5

Nebraska C2
Nevada A2
New Hampshire F2
New Jersey F2
New Mexico B3–C3
New Orleans D4
New York City F2
New York State E2–F2
North Carolina F3
North Dakota C1

Ohio E2
Oklahoma C3
Oregon A1

Pacific Ocean A3–A5
Pennsylvania E2–F2
Puerto Rico C5

Rhode Island F2

San Francisco A2
South Carolina E3
South Dakota C2

Tennessee E3
Texas C3–C4

Utah B2

Vermont F1–F2
Virginia F2

Washington, D.C. F2
Washington State A1
West Virginia E2
Wisconsin D2
Wyoming B2–C2

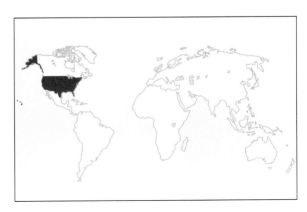

Quick Facts

Official Name   The United States of America

Capital   Washington, D.C.

Official Language   English

Population   272 million

Land area   3,717,796 square miles (9,629,092 square km) — all 50 states

States   Alabama, Alaska, Arizona, Arkansas, California, Colorado, Connecticut, Delaware, Florida, Georgia, Hawaii, Idaho, Illinois, Indiana, Iowa, Kansas, Kentucky, Louisiana, Maine, Maryland, Massachusetts, Michigan, Minnesota, Mississippi, Missouri, Montana, Nebraska, Nevada, New Hampshire, New Jersey, New Mexico, New York, North Carolina, North Dakota, Ohio, Oklahoma, Oregon, Pennsylvania, Rhode Island, South Carolina, South Dakota, Tennessee, Texas, Utah, Vermont, Virginia, Washington, West Virginia, Wisconsin, Wyoming

Famous Leaders   George Washington, Thomas Jefferson, Abraham Lincoln

Currency   U.S. Dollar

Opposite: Many villages in New England date back to before the Revolutionary War.

Glossary

abstract expressionism: a popular art movement, after World War II, that used patterns and shapes, instead of actual people and objects, to express thoughts and emotions.

adaptability: the ability to adjust to new situations.

advocated: supported a cause publicly.

commercialism: the practice of making large profits from something, without a regard for quality.

contiguous: next to or touching.

criticism: the act of expressing disapproval of people or objects.

debilitating: causing to weaken.

deciduous: related to trees that shed leaves seasonally.

deterioration: worsening; the lowering of value or quality.

extended families: family groups that include both a nuclear family and other close relatives, all living together in the same household.

Great Depression: a time of terrible economic problems around the world, beginning with the U.S. stock market crash in 1929 and ending with the start of World War II.

grits: boiled, ground cornmeal served as a breakfast cereal or side dish.

improvisation: the act of doing something without advance planning or preparation.

incorporated: two or more individual parts combined to make one larger unit.

indigenous: originating in a particular country or place.

individuality: personal identity; the qualities that make a person different from others.

irrigation: the supply of water by artificial means.

kosher food: food that is in keeping with Jewish dietary laws.

linguistic: related to language.

media: means of communication.

novel: new and unusual.

nuclear families: family groups made up of two parents and their children.

post-modernism: an art movement in the late twentieth century that rejected modern art in favor of more traditional styles and techniques.

reservations: acres of land set aside for use by Native Americans.

More Books to Read

The African American Civil Rights Movement. Causes and Consequences series. Michael Weber (Raintree/Steck Vaughn)

American Civil War: A House Divided. Edward F. Dolan (Millbrook Press)

American Fairy Tales: From Rip Van Winkle to the Rootabaga Stories. Neil Philip (Disney Press)

The American Revolution. World History series. Bonnie L. Lukes (Lucent Books)

The Declaration of Independence. Cornerstones of Freedom series. Richard Conrad Stein (Children's Press)

The First Americans. History of U.S. series. Joy Hakim (Oxford University Press)

USA. Festivals of the World series. Elizabeth Berg (Gareth Stevens)

The World of Native Americans. The World of series. Marion Wood (Peter Bedrick Books)

Videos

California/Hawaii/Alaska: American Roadtrips. (Questar Inc.)

Native American History. (TMW Media Group)

United States. (Questar Inc.)

United States Presidents Box Set. (IVN Entertainment)

Web Sites

www.50states.com/

www.odci.gov/cia/publications/ factbook/us.html

www.usahistory.com/presidents/

cube.ice.net/~edbear/USfacts.html

Due to the dynamic nature of the Internet, some web sites stay current longer than others. To find additional web sites about the United States, use a reliable search engine and enter one or more of the following keywords: *baseball, California, Hollywood, Abraham Lincoln, Native Americans, New York, George Washington.*

Index